MW01341435

Restaurant Personality

Thank You

To my family, who are pillars of optimism in the face of adversity.
Your encouragement of creativity continues to inspire and
appreciate in the goodness of life.

To my Mom and Dad for their continuous support.
Their constant dedication to the needs of others is evident
in the fortunes of gratitude.

And for the many personalities of the world
that make this life unique.

Thank You

First Edition

Published in the United States in 2008 by
Sleep Tree Publishing Company
P.O. Box 9262
Charlotte, NC 28299
www.sleeptighttonight.com

Copyright © 2007 by Stephen C. Healy

All rights reserved. No part of this publication may be reproduced or transmitted in any form or by any means, electronic or mechanical, including photocopy, recording, or any information storage or retrieval system now known or to be invented without permission in writing from the publisher.

ISBN: 978-0-9798947-1-8

Restaurant Personality
Restaurant Personality
ANYTIME
DAY
OR
NIGHT

Welcome, Welcome to Restaurant Personality!
Come in, Come in... do not be shy. Here we serve any type,
everything from Upset to Polite,
at any time of day,
at any time of night.

Come in, Come in...
the menu is set for all people alike,
to each an order of personality and
for each personality
an appetite.

Our Cook has different recipes you see. Tastes can differ so you must choose who you'll be, by what you eat. It all depends upon your mood.

Remember though, that comfort thoughts make comfort food.

Come in, Come in to Restaurant Personality,
where meals are not meals,
like fish, chicken or steers.
They are meals of moods renamed for foods,
but they feed us all the same.

Sit down, Sit down, and look through the menu please.
But do keep in mind that, as we all find,
personalities are sure to change.

We have put together a lovely spread of delicious personalities to butter your bread.

There are so many plates of traits and tastes that make no mistake you will leave well fed.

Every order comes with a side of character on a stick.

We call them characteristics and you can eat as many as you like, as long as they don't make you sick.

Spite can be a common meal.
It isn't prepared any time of day
well.

It's usually thick, but thins out
quite quick with just a deep
breath of fresh air.

Today I recommend a much lighter meal, something that keeps you one step ahead of your heel — a warm Smile of Wishes served over stewed happy greens, we call Dreams. It's a great way to start your day, eating these things.

You could begin with Regret or some Stress To Do's.
But piling a plate of Stress with To Do's
may be too much for you, and Regret
often gives you the blues.

In fact, the filet of Regret you'll never forget,
but the more you eat, the more you'll get.
You will be so filled with what was and what is,
that once is enough to never want it again.

If you want a choice, this is just my voice,
but the Selfless Delight is a true morning blue.

It tastes like the sun's light, so unforgettably good that
you'll be looking forward to the new day
by the end of the night.

The Curiosity Tray is quite a treat.

You never know what you're going to eat,
but there are enough personality traits
to put together a feast.

Anger can be too hot to eat, so the flavor is often charred.

And a serving of Greed is nothing to feed for you will be filled full with things you don't need.

Happiness is an all you can eat dish.
It is rich, but light, and prepared just right.

Feel free to stuff your face, as long as
you don't take a piece from someone else's plate.

Jealousy has a bitter taste, because it's never the meal that you want. It has a smell that will make you drool, but is often the meal of fools.

Resentment is very similar, although the serving is made from spoiled food.

Even if you don't order a plate of Sadness,
it will sometimes be served to you.
It's a food you never get used to.

Sadness is often wet and soggy
and either eaten with a spoon, or
by sticking your face right in.
It's not always bad though
and usually goes away
pretty soon.

The Cutlet of Love is a divine entree.
You don't need a knife for this slice of life, because it is soft and sweet.

Love melts in your mouth,
no taste bud left out,
leaving your belly complete.

And last, but not least is the restaurant's specialty.
The Personality Stew is a combination of dishes
made from the Cook's wishes,
and it's guaranteed to be delicious.

For in the stew you will see a
reflection that can only be true
to the person in you.

It is not bitter or harsh, but crave for more you will. It
has the taste to put a smile on your face
before you are done with the meal.

I also suggest,
if you choose to get stew,
that you share it with others.
And when you do,
it will taste better to you!

There are other dishes of course,
but place the order that
suits you best.

Each person has an appetite
for personality and the
menu is set.

Thank you,
Thank you,
enjoy your dining
experience at
Restaurant Personality!
If you do not order what you want this time,
change your frame of mind
and we'll see you tomorrow
at any time of day,
at any time of night.

"By the first star you see at night
and the wish I may's
and the wish I might's...

May you find this wish
I wish for you...

That you sleep tight tonight
and tomorrow night too!"

Getting to Know

Sleep Tree Publishing Co.

Sleep Tree Publishing Co. is dedicated to imagination. The several branches that make up Sleep Tree are unique, but each stems from the trunk of creativity. It's founder used to climb trees as a boy. There he would write stories and poems with a branch and a pen. And although the company is relatively new, the roots have long been in place. As Sleep Tree grows, we hope that you climb with us.

Branching Out
Divisions of Sleep Tree Publishing Co.

Sleep Tight Tonight develops innovative children's literature for both parent and child.

Bean Table prints coffee table books, as well as a selected number of custom publications.

Because She Said So offers timeless greeting cards, with the meaningful and appropriately emotional gift of words.

Thank you for supporting Sleep Tree Publishing Co. We will continue to create quality products that are inspired by imagination.